The Basics Of Cybersecurity

by John Christly, CISSP

Table of Contents

About the Author

John Christly, CISSP, CFE, LSSMBB

https://www.linkedin.com/in/johnchristly/

With three decades of dedicated service in the ever-evolving realm of Information Technology and Cybersecurity, John Christly stands as a beacon of expertise and innovation in safeguarding digital landscapes.

A business professional who is also armed with industry certifications including the presligious **CISSP** (Certified Information Systems Security Professional), the **CFE** (Certified Fraud Examiner), and the revered **Lean Six Sigma Master Black Belt**, John has honed a skill set that blends technical prowess with strategic acumen.

Throughout his career, John has traversed the complex terrain of cybersecurity, emerging as a trusted advisor to organizations worldwide. From fortifying network defenses against emerging threats to architecting resilient infrastructures, he has remained at the forefront of technological advancements.

Beyond his technical proficiency, John possesses a rare ability to distill intricate concepts into actionable insights, making his expertise accessible to both novices and seasoned professionals alike.

In "The Basics of Cybersecurity," John delves deep into his wealth of experience, offering readers invaluable perspectives garnered from the frontlines of cyber defense.

Whether you're an aspiring cybersecurity professional, a seasoned veteran seeking to stay ahead of the curve, or a business leader navigating the complexities of digital security, this book promises to be an indispensable guide on your journey through the digital frontier.

Some words from John Christly...

Hello and welcome to my book! I am glad you have found this publication.

Developing this book was truly a labor of love for me. I am very proud to be able to share it with you. Please share it with your family, friends, and co-workers.

This book would not have been possible without the unwavering support provided by my wife Carolyn and my daughter Olivia. They are the foundations in my life!

Those that know me well know that I am a passionate IT and cybersecurity professional.

With a background in military service and a deep understanding of industry regulations, I bring a unique perspective to the IT and cybersecurity landscape.

I have been "in the trenches" for many years now serving in key roles such as CIO, CISO, and CTO, and helping organizations of all sizes to build resilient IT systems, fortify their security systems, and grow security related practice offerings.

I also own my own consulting company and have been fortunate to help many customers over the years with issues that they needed help with.

My experience includes several industry regulations and standards including HIPAA, HITECH, HITRUST, CMMC, CJIS, ISO 27001, FERPA, FIPA, GDPR, NIST 800-171, NIST 800-53, SOX, NY DFS, and PCI.

My dedication extends beyond my work, as evidenced by my numerous certifications and ongoing commitment to learning.

 I enjoy sharing my knowledge, whether it's through teaching, speaking at events, or writing books or material for industry publications.

I welcome you to connect with me on LinkedIn or check out my website at **https://omcsystems.com** where you will find links to my podcast series, links to my courses on Udemy, and ways to contact me if you need consulting help.

Thanks again for being here.

I truly hope you enjoy my book. - John

Introduction to Cybersecurity

Cybersecurity is a critical aspect of modern technology and business operations, encompassing a broad spectrum of tools and practices aimed at protecting digital assets from a wide range of threats. As our society becomes increasingly reliant on digital systems and networks, ensuring the **confidentiality, integrity, and availability** of sensitive information has never been more important. The potential consequences of a cybersecurity breach extend far beyond financial losses, encompassing damage to reputation, loss of customer trust, and even legal implications.

Confidentiality serves as the foundation of cybersecurity, ensuring that only authorized individuals have access to sensitive data. This principle is upheld through various means, such as encryption, access controls, and secure communication protocols. **Integrity**, on the other hand, focuses on maintaining the accuracy and consistency of data, preventing unauthorized modifications or tampering. **Availability** completes the triad by ensuring that information and resources are accessible when needed, without disruptions or downtime.

A robust cybersecurity strategy requires a multi-layered approach that combines technology, processes, and people.

Network security plays a crucial role in safeguarding digital infrastructure, with measures such as firewalls, intrusion detection systems, and secure network architecture.

Endpoint security focuses on securing individual devices, such as laptops and smartphones, against malware, unauthorized access, and other threats.

Access control mechanisms, such as strong authentication and role-based access, help control who can access what data within an organization.

Data encryption is a fundamental tool for protecting information both at rest and in transit, making it unreadable to unauthorized parties.

Security awareness training is a key component of any cybersecurity program, as human error remains one of the most significant vulnerabilities in organizations. By educating employees on best practices, recognizing phishing attempts, and understanding the importance of data security, organizations can significantly enhance their overall security posture.

In addition to preventative measures, a proactive approach to cybersecurity requires **continuous monitoring, threat intelligence analysis, and rapid incident response**.

Advanced technologies like artificial intelligence and machine learning are increasingly being used to detect and respond to cyber threats in real time, enhancing the effectiveness of cybersecurity operations.

As the cybersecurity landscape continues to evolve, organizations must stay informed about emerging threats, regulatory requirements, and best practices in cybersecurity.

By investing in cybersecurity measures, businesses can mitigate risks, protect their assets, and maintain the trust of their stakeholders in an increasingly interconnected world.

Understanding the Threat Landscape

Cybersecurity in the modern digital landscape is a critical concern for individuals and organizations as they navigate a complex and rapidly evolving threat landscape.

The proliferation of technology and connectivity has created a myriad of opportunities for cybercriminals to exploit vulnerabilities and launch attacks for financial gain, data theft, and other nefarious activities.

As organizations strive to secure their digital assets and protect sensitive information, understanding the concept of the attack surface becomes indispensable in assessing and mitigating cybersecurity risks effectively.

The attack surface encompasses all potential entry points that threat actors can target to infiltrate systems, exfiltrate data, or disrupt operations. It comprises a wide range of assets, including hardware, software, networks, applications, and even human elements such as employees or third-party vendors. By conducting a comprehensive analysis of their attack surface, organizations can identify vulnerabilities, prioritize security measures, and fortify their defenses against potential cyber threats. This holistic approach enables organizations to develop a robust cybersecurity strategy that addresses all facets of the attack surface and reduces the risk of successful attacks.

Cyber threats continue to evolve in sophistication and complexity, posing significant challenges to traditional security measures. Threat actors employ a variety of tactics, techniques, and procedures (TTPs) to breach defenses, including advanced persistent threats (APTs), zero-day exploits, social engineering, and insider threats. These tactics are designed to evade detection, bypass security controls, and compromise systems, underscoring the need for organizations to remain vigilant and adaptive in their cybersecurity efforts.

To effectively combat these evolving threats, organizations must adopt a multi-faceted cybersecurity approach that combines advanced technologies, threat intelligence sharing, proactive monitoring, and comprehensive employee training.

Leveraging tools such as firewalls, intrusion detection systems, endpoint protection, and encryption mechanisms can help organizations detect, prevent, and respond to cyber attacks in real-time.

Regular security assessments, penetration testing, and incident response planning are essential components of a strong cybersecurity posture that can enhance resilience and preparedness against threats.

A deep understanding of the intricate threat landscape, combined with a proactive and comprehensive cybersecurity strategy, is vital for protecting critical assets and mitigating cyber risks.

By integrating advanced technologies, robust policies, and proactive cybersecurity practices, organizations can strengthen their security posture and safeguard sensitive information from malicious actors in an increasingly interconnected digital environment.

By staying informed, vigilant, and adaptable, organizations can navigate the complexities of cybersecurity challenges and safeguard their digital assets effectively.

Common Cybersecurity Challenges

In today's interconnected digital landscape, organizations face a myriad of cybersecurity challenges that demand a proactive and adaptive approach to fortify their defenses against evolving threats. The escalating sophistication of cyber threats compels organizations to remain vigilant and agile in safeguarding their data and systems. Cybercriminals, driven by financial gain or malicious intent, continuously exploit vulnerabilities in networks and devices, necessitating robust security measures to mitigate risks effectively.

One of the paramount challenges confronting organizations is the acute shortage of skilled cybersecurity professionals. The industry-wide talent gap poses a critical barrier to enhancing security postures, leaving organizations vulnerable to cyber risks.

To address this issue, organizations must invest in attracting and nurturing cybersecurity talent through training programs, partnerships with educational institutions, and the cultivation of a culture that values cybersecurity expertise. By prioritizing talent development, organizations can augment their cybersecurity capabilities and better defend against cyber threats.

The complexity of modern IT environments presents a formidable obstacle for organizations seeking to bolster their cybersecurity defenses. The proliferation of cloud services, IoT devices, and interconnected systems has expanded the attack surface, creating challenges in monitoring and securing diverse technologies effectively.

Protecting against threats in such a dynamic ecosystem necessitates a comprehensive approach that integrates network security, endpoint protection, access management, and threat intelligence.

By adopting an integrated security strategy, organizations can enhance their resilience against cyber threats and mitigate potential vulnerabilities across their technological infrastructure.

Moreover, regulatory compliance adds another layer of complexity to cybersecurity initiatives, particularly for industries subject to stringent data protection laws and regulations.

Ensuring compliance with industry-specific mandates requires organizations to align their cybersecurity practices with regulatory requirements, conduct regular assessments, and implement robust policies and controls to safeguard sensitive information effectively. By proactively addressing compliance obligations, organizations can reduce legal risks, enhance data security, and build trust with stakeholders.

In light of these multifaceted cybersecurity challenges, organizations must prioritize risk assessment, threat detection, incident response, and continuous improvement within their cybersecurity strategies.

By investing in cybersecurity talent and technology, staying informed about emerging threats, streamlining security measures, and ensuring compliance with regulations, organizations can enhance their cyber resilience and safeguard their critical assets in an increasingly hostile digital landscape.

Adopting a proactive and holistic approach to cybersecurity is paramount in today's rapidly evolving threat landscape, where organizations must adapt and innovate to protect their digital assets and maintain operational continuity.

Principles of Secure Authentication and

Multi-Factor Authentication (MFA)

In the ever-evolving landscape of cybersecurity, the imperative nature of robust and secure authentication mechanisms cannot be overstated. At the core of safeguarding sensitive data and thwarting unauthorized access lies the critical role played by authentication protocols. In this context, **Multi-Factor Authentication (MFA)** emerges as a pivotal tool in the arsenal of cybersecurity strategies, transcending conventional authentication paradigms to fortify defenses against a multitude of threats that loom in the digital realm.

Multi-Factor Authentication embodies a multi-layered approach to identity verification, necessitating users to provide multiple forms of authentication to validate their identity. This multifaceted framework typically comprises elements categorized into three distinct factors: something the user knows, exemplified by passwords or Personal Identification Numbers (PINs); something the user possesses, such as mobile devices, security tokens, or smart cards; and finally, something the user is, characterized by biometric markers like fingerprints, iris scans, or facial recognition technology.

The fundamental strength of Multi-Factor Authentication lies in its intrinsic capability to introduce complexity and resilience into the authentication process. By mandating the provision of multiple factors to ascertain identity, MFA stands as a formidable barrier against unauthorized access attempts.

In scenarios where one authentication factor is compromised, the multi-layered approach of MFA acts as a robust deterrent, substantially raising the bar for cyber adversaries seeking to breach security defenses. This strategic elevation significantly mitigates the risks associated with prevalent cyber threats, including but not limited to brute force attacks, credential stuffing, and password-based exploits.

Furthermore, the adoption of Multi-Factor Authentication not only bolsters cybersecurity postures but also aligns organizations with statutory regulations and compliance standards that govern data protection and privacy.

Regulatory frameworks such as the General Data Protection Regulation (GDPR) and the Health Insurance Portability and Accountability Act (HIPAA) mandate the implementation of stringent security measures, including robust authentication protocols, to safeguard confidential information.

By embracing MFA, organizations demonstrate a commitment to adhering to these regulatory directives, ensuring the safeguarding of sensitive data and fostering trust with stakeholders.

It is **vitally important** to ensure that you have MFA enabled *everywhere and anywhere* you can on all of your accounts. This includes online banking accounts, your kids college portals, your e-mail web portals, and anywhere else that you have a login to a web portal where MFA is able to be turned on and used.

The strategic integration of Multi-Factor Authentication in organizational cybersecurity frameworks epitomizes a proactive stance towards fortifying security postures, diminishing risks, and fostering a culture of vigilance and accountability in protecting critical assets.

By prioritizing secure authentication practices, organizations not only enhance their resilience against cyber threats but also signal a steadfast dedication to upholding data integrity, confidentiality, and compliance with prevailing regulatory mandates.

Importance of Patch Management

Patch management is an essential aspect of cybersecurity management for businesses and organizations of all sizes. The process involves the timely identification, assessment, prioritization, testing, and deployment of security patches to address vulnerabilities in software, operating systems, and applications. By proactively managing patches, organizations can fortify their defenses against cyber threats and reduce their exposure to potential security breaches and data compromises.

It is crucial to recognize that cyber threats are continuously evolving, and cybercriminals are constantly seeking to exploit vulnerabilities in software and systems to gain unauthorized access and steal sensitive information. Security patches issued by software vendors are designed to plug these vulnerabilities and protect systems from exploitation. Therefore, a **robust patch management strategy** is imperative for maintaining the security and integrity of an organization's digital assets.

One of the primary advantages of effective patch management is its ability to enhance the overall security posture of an organization. By ensuring that systems are up to date with the latest patches, businesses can significantly reduce the attack surface available to malicious actors and mitigate the risk of security incidents. This proactive approach to security maintenance not only safeguards sensitive data but also helps to preserve the organization's credibility and reputation in the event of a cyber attack.

In practice, patch management involves a systematic and well-defined process that begins with the identification of vulnerabilities through security assessments, monitoring security advisories, and leveraging threat intelligence resources.

Once vulnerabilities are identified, patches are prioritized based on severity and criticality to the organization's infrastructure and operations. Thorough testing of patches in a controlled environment is essential to ensure that the updates do not introduce new issues or disrupt the functionality of systems.

Automated patch management tools can greatly streamline the patching process by automating the detection, deployment, and monitoring of patches across the organization's IT environment. These tools help organizations stay current with security updates and minimize the window of opportunity for attackers to exploit known vulnerabilities.

Additionally, regular audits and reporting mechanisms can provide visibility into patch compliance levels and help track progress in maintaining a secure and well-protected IT environment.

Apart from bolstering cybersecurity defenses, effective patch management also plays a vital role in regulatory compliance.

Many industry regulations and data protection laws mandate the timely application of security patches to safeguard sensitive information and maintain the confidentiality, integrity, and availability of data.

Organizations that fail to adhere to these requirements may face legal consequences, financial penalties, and reputational damage.

Ways to keep your systems up to date.

In today's interconnected digital world, ensuring the security of our devices and data is paramount. One crucial aspect of this is keeping our operating systems up to date to protect against vulnerabilities.

Additionally, being vigilant against suspicious activities such as phishing attempts is essential. In these next sections, we'll explore how to enable automatic updates on both Windows and macOS systems, how to keep certain 3rd party applications up to date, and how to report suspicious events to the relevant authorities such as the Federal Communications Commission (FCC).

Why Automatic Updates Are Important:

1. Security: Cyber threats evolve rapidly, and software vulnerabilities are frequently exploited by attackers. Automatic updates ensure that critical security patches are applied promptly, reducing the window of vulnerability for potential exploitation.

2. Stability: Updates often include bug fixes and performance enhancements that contribute to the stability and smooth functioning of the software. By staying up-to-date, users can avoid encountering compatibility issues or system crashes caused by outdated software versions.

3. Convenience: Manually checking for updates and applying them can be time-consuming and prone to oversight. Automatic updates alleviate this burden by handling the update process in the background, requiring minimal user intervention.

4. Compliance: In certain industries or organizations, compliance requirements mandate the timely application of security patches and updates. Enabling automatic updates helps ensure adherence to these standards without the need for manual oversight.

Enabling Automatic Updates on Windows

Windows operating systems offer automatic updates to ensure that your system is always equipped with the latest security patches and features. Here's how you can enable this feature:

1. Access Windows Update Settings: Click on the Start button, then navigate to Settings > Update & Security.

2. Configure Update Settings: In the Update & Security window, select Windows Update from the left-hand menu. Here, you can configure various update settings. Ensure that "Automatic (recommended)" is selected under the "Choose when updates are installed" section.

3. Advanced Options: For further customization, click on "Advanced options." Here, you can specify additional settings such as the ability to defer updates or receive updates for other Microsoft products.

4. Restart Options: Windows may require a restart after installing updates. Under "Restart options," you can choose when to schedule these restarts to minimize disruption.

5. Check for Updates: Although automatic updates are enabled, you can still manually check for updates by clicking the "Check for updates" button in the Windows Update settings.

Enabling Automatic Updates on macOS

Similar to Windows, macOS also offers automatic update functionality to keep your system secure and up to date. Here's how you can enable it:

1. Access System Preferences: Click on the Apple menu at the top-left corner of the screen and select "System Preferences."

2. Open Software Update: In the System Preferences window, click on "Software Update." This will open the Software Update settings.

3. Enable Automatic Updates: Check the box next to "Automatically keep my Mac up to date." This will ensure that your macOS system receives automatic updates.

4. Customize Update Settings: You can customize which types of updates your Mac automatically installs by clicking on "Advanced." Here, you can choose to install macOS updates, app updates, and system data files automatically.

5. Check for Updates Manually: Even with automatic updates enabled, you can manually check for updates by clicking the "Check Now" button in the Software Update settings.

Enabling Automatic Updates for Third-Party Products

In today's interconnected digital landscape, where cyber threats loom large and software vulnerabilities abound, ensuring the security and stability of **third-party products** is paramount. Among these, applications like Adobe Acrobat and Java (among many others) play vital roles in countless systems worldwide. However, their widespread usage also makes them prime targets for malicious actors seeking to exploit vulnerabilities for nefarious purposes.

One of the most effective measures users can take to protect themselves against such threats is to **enable automatic updates** for these third-party products.

Automatic updates streamline the process of applying patches and security fixes, ensuring that systems remain fortified against the latest threats without requiring manual intervention.

In this next section, we'll delve into the steps for enabling automatic updates for Adobe Acrobat and Java, as two examples of how this can be done.

(Note, steps to enable updates in products you use may vary by software vendor and application vendor).

Enabling Automatic Updates for Adobe Acrobat:

1. Open Adobe Acrobat: Launch the Adobe Acrobat application on your computer.

2. Navigate to Preferences: Click on the "Edit" menu (or the Acrobat menu on macOS), then select "Preferences."

3. Access Update Settings: In the Preferences dialog box, locate and click on the "Updater" category on the left-hand side.

4. Enable Automatic Updates: Within the Updater settings, ensure that the "Automatically install updates" option is checked. You may also choose to specify the frequency of update checks and installations according to your preferences.

5. Confirm Settings: Click "OK" or "Apply" to save your changes and exit the Preferences dialog box.

Enabling Automatic Updates for Java:

1. Open Java Control Panel: Access the Java Control Panel by searching for "Java" in the Windows Start menu and selecting the appropriate option.

2. Navigate to Update Tab: In the Java Control Panel, navigate to the "Update" tab at the top.

3. Adjust Update Settings: Under the "Automatic Update" section, select the option to "Check for Updates Automatically" and choose whether you want Java to install updates automatically or prompt you before installation.

4. Save Changes: Click "Apply" or "OK" to save your settings and exit the Java Control Panel.

Enabling automatic updates for third-party products such as Adobe Acrobat and Java is a simple yet essential practice for safeguarding the security, stability, and compliance of systems. By staying proactive in keeping software up-to-date, users can mitigate risks posed by cyber threats and enjoy a smoother, more secure computing experience.

Patch management (and 3rd party application updates) are **fundamental pillars of cybersecurity** that demand attention and diligence from organizations seeking to safeguard their digital assets and maintain a strong security posture.

By establishing a comprehensive patch management program, prioritizing security updates, leveraging automated tools, and adhering to industry best practices, organizations can mitigate security risks, enhance operational resilience, and demonstrate a commitment to protecting their data and stakeholders from potential cyber threats.

Implementing Effective Firewall Protection

Firewalls stand as an essential component in the realm of cybersecurity, serving as the primary barrier between networks and potential threats. The selection of the appropriate firewall type is a critical decision that shapes the overall security posture of an organization.

Network firewalls, with their ability to inspect and control traffic based on network-layer information, provide fundamental protection against a wide array of malicious activities. In contrast, application firewalls offer granular control over specific applications, enabling organizations to enforce more stringent security policies at the application layer.

Unified Threat Management (UTM) systems represent a comprehensive approach to network security, integrating multiple security features into a single solution. UTM platforms encompass functionalities such as intrusion detection and prevention, antivirus protection, content filtering, and virtual private networking (VPN), offering a holistic defense strategy against diverse cyber threats.

The meticulous configuration of firewall rules is imperative in aligning security measures with organizational objectives and compliance requirements. Access control lists define the traffic that is allowed or blocked based on criteria such as source and destination IP addresses, ports, and protocols. Regular audits of firewall configurations facilitate the identification of misconfigurations or outdated rules, enabling organizations to maintain an effective defense posture and swiftly adapt to evolving security challenges.

Continuous monitoring of network traffic is critical for swiftly identifying and mitigating security incidents. Intrusion detection systems (IDS) embedded within firewalls actively monitor network traffic for suspicious patterns and behaviors, generating alerts for potential security issues. Analyzing firewall logs and security event data provides organizations with valuable insights into network activity, facilitating proactive threat hunting and incident response actions.

The maintenance of firewall integrity relies on a proactive approach to patch management and firmware updates. Security patches released by firewall vendors address known vulnerabilities and strengthen security defenses against emerging threats. Establishing a regular maintenance schedule ensures that firewalls are up to date with the latest security enhancements, reducing the attack surface and enhancing overall protection.

Incorporating additional security layers, such as Intrusion Detection and Prevention Systems (IDPS) and Security Information and Event Management (SIEM) solutions, can complement firewall defenses. IDPS solutions offer advanced threat detection capabilities and automated response mechanisms, enhancing the overall security posture. SIEM platforms aggregate and correlate security event data from multiple sources, providing organizations with comprehensive visibility into security incidents and facilitating timely response measures.

In essence, effective firewall management is essential in fortifying network security and safeguarding sensitive data against cyber threats. By embracing a multi-faceted approach, encompassing careful firewall selection, meticulous configuration, diligent monitoring, proactive maintenance, and integrated security solutions, organizations can bolster their defenses and stay resilient in the face of evolving cyber threats.

A well-orchestrated firewall strategy, bolstered by supplementary security measures, is paramount in the dynamic landscape of cybersecurity.

Recognizing and Defending Against Phishing Attacks

Phishing attacks continue to represent a pervasive and ever-evolving threat in the realm of cybersecurity, exploiting the vulnerabilities of individuals and organizations by leveraging deceptive tactics to compromise sensitive information and financial security.

As technology advances and cybercriminals become increasingly sophisticated in their approaches, it is imperative for all stakeholders to cultivate a comprehensive understanding of phishing attacks and implement robust defense mechanisms to mitigate potential harm effectively.

Email phishing, one of the most prevalent forms of phishing attacks, remains a primary vector for cybercriminals seeking to gain unauthorized access to valuable information. These fraudulent emails often masquerade as legitimate communications from trusted sources, employing various social engineering techniques to manipulate recipients into divulging confidential information or clicking on malicious links. To combat email phishing effectively, individuals must adopt a discerning mindset, meticulously scrutinizing sender addresses for anomalies, conducting thorough assessments of email content for inconsistencies or grammatical errors, and resisting the urge to interact with suspicious elements.

Spear phishing, a more targeted and personalized form of phishing, poses an increased risk due to its tailored approach that leverages specific details about individuals or organizations to enhance credibility and deception. By utilizing personal information to craft elaborate schemes, cybercriminals can circumvent traditional security measures and establish a sense of trust with their intended victims. Mitigating the risks associated with spear phishing requires individuals to adopt a proactive stance on data privacy, limit the dissemination of personal information online, and implement stringent verification processes to authenticate the legitimacy of digital communications.

In addition to email-based threats, phishing attacks can manifest through alternative channels such as **text messages, social media platforms, or phone calls,** expanding the attack surface and necessitating heightened security awareness across all communication mediums. Individuals must exercise caution when interacting with unsolicited messages, diligently verifying the identities of senders before providing any sensitive information, and promptly reporting any suspicious activities to relevant authorities to prevent potential compromises.

For organizations, the implementation of robust cybersecurity measures is paramount to defend against phishing attacks effectively. This includes deploying advanced email filtering solutions to identify and block malicious content, integrating secure email authentication mechanisms (like SPF and DKIM) to validate sender authenticity, and establishing clear incident response protocols to mitigate the impact of successful attacks swiftly. Furthermore, ongoing employee training programs and simulated phishing exercises can enhance workforce resilience to social engineering tactics, fostering a culture of cyber awareness and vigilance within the organizational environment.

Combating phishing attacks demands a multi-faceted and proactive approach that encompasses technological safeguards, user education, and strategic risk management initiatives.

By promoting a culture of cybersecurity awareness, leveraging cutting-edge defense mechanisms, and maintaining a vigilant stance against fraudulent practices, individuals and organizations can fortify their defenses against phishing threats and safeguard the integrity of their digital assets.

Securing Data and Privacy

In today's interconnected and data-centric landscape, the imperative to safeguard data and preserve privacy has never been more critical. The proliferation of digital platforms, cloud services, and remote working environments has significantly expanded the attack surface for cyber threats and data breaches, necessitating a comprehensive and robust approach to information security.

Encryption stands as a cornerstone of data protection, forming the bedrock of confidentiality mechanisms that organizations rely on to secure their sensitive information. By leveraging advanced encryption algorithms and technologies, organizations can transform plaintext data into ciphertext, rendering it indecipherable to unauthorized entities. Encryption ensures that data remains confidential and secure, whether it is in transit across networks or at rest within storage systems, providing an essential layer of defense against unauthorized access and data breaches.

Access controls are essential components of a data security strategy, enabling organizations to enforce the principle of least privilege and restrict access to sensitive data based on user roles and responsibilities. By implementing robust authentication mechanisms, authorization protocols, and user permissions, organizations can effectively manage user access to data resources, mitigating the risk of unauthorized data disclosures and internal threats. Granular access controls help organizations maintain data integrity, confidentiality, and availability, thereby enhancing overall security posture.

Regular data backups and comprehensive disaster recovery planning are vital aspects of data security preparedness, enabling organizations to mitigate the impact of data loss or corruption due to cyber incidents, natural disasters, or system failures. Data backups serve as a crucial lifeline for restoring lost information and ensuring business continuity in the face of unforeseen disruptions.

Well-designed disaster recovery plans outline clear procedures for **incident response, recovery efforts, and communication strategies**, enabling organizations to minimize downtime, recover quickly, and protect their data assets from potential threats.

Compliance with data protection regulations is a fundamental requirement for organizations operating in today's regulatory environment, where privacy laws and regulations impose stringent requirements for protecting personal data and maintaining data security.

Regulations such as the **General Data Protection Regulation (GDPR)**, the **Health Insurance Portability and Accountability Act (HIPAA), Payment Card Industry (PCI)**, and others mandate data protection standards, breach notification requirements, and privacy safeguards to safeguard the rights and privacy of individuals.

Adhering to these regulations not only helps organizations build trust with customers and stakeholders but also shields them from legal repercussions, financial penalties, and reputational damage stemming from non-compliance.

The regulatory landscape governing data privacy and protection continues to evolve, with stringent regulations such as GDPR and CCPA establishing clear mandates for organizations to safeguard personal data and uphold individuals' privacy rights.

Compliance with data protection laws necessitates the implementation of robust data security measures, privacy impact assessments, and transparent data processing practices to mitigate legal risks, financial liabilities, and reputational damage resulting from non-compliance.

By adhering to stringent privacy regulations and fostering a culture of data protection, organizations can instill trust among consumers, engendering long-term relationships built on transparent data management practices.

A holistic approach to securing data and privacy encompasses **encryption, access controls, data backup, disaster recovery planning, and regulatory compliance**.

By adopting best practices in data security, organizations can fortify their defenses against cyber threats, demonstrate a commitment to protecting sensitive information, and uphold the trust and expectations of their stakeholders in an era of pervasive digital risks.

Incident Response and Recovery

In the dynamic realm of cybersecurity, the discipline of **incident response and recovery** holds paramount importance as a cornerstone in fortifying organizational resilience against the relentless onslaught of cyber threats.

An organization's capability to respond to security incidents swiftly and effectively is not just a reactive measure but a strategic imperative that demands meticulous planning, rapid execution, and continuous refinement to counteract the evolving tactics of threat actors and safeguard critical assets.

The initial phase of incident response revolves around the vital aspects of **detection and identification**. Prompt detection of security incidents is pivotal in curtailing their impact and preventing further escalation. Utilizing advanced monitoring tools, intrusion detection systems, and Security Information and Event Management (SIEM) solutions, organizations can proactively identify anomalous activities and potential threats, enabling security teams to mount a timely and targeted response to mitigate risks and protect sensitive data.

Transitioning from detection to **response** necessitates a swift and decisive shift in focus towards containment and mitigation efforts. By swiftly isolating affected systems, cutting off potential threat vectors, and implementing proactive measures to thwart further compromise, organizations can limit the scope of the incident and minimize the disruption to critical operations and services. The agility and effectiveness of the response are critical factors in mitigating the potential damage and restoring normalcy swiftly.

The **investigative phase** following containment is crucial in unraveling the intricacies of the incident, understanding the root causes, and reconstructing the sequence of events to thwart future threats effectively. Through thorough forensic analysis, examination of compromised systems, and gathering threat intelligence, organizations can derive valuable insights to bolster their defenses, address underlying vulnerabilities, and fortify their security posture against persistent and emerging threats.

The **recovery phase** post-incident is dedicated to restoring affected systems and data to operational functionality securely and expediently. Leveraging robust backup and recovery mechanisms, implementing security patches and updates, and reinforcing security controls are essential steps in mitigating residual risks, enhancing resilience, and preventing the recurrence of similar incidents. Organizations must prioritize the restoration of services while maintaining a keen focus on security to prevent re-exploitation of vulnerabilities by threat actors.

Clear and effective communication plays a pivotal role in successful incident response and recovery efforts. Transparent and timely communication with internal stakeholders, senior management, legal counsel, insurance providers, regulatory bodies, customers, and other relevant parties fosters trust, cooperation, and coordinated response efforts, ensuring alignment, compliance, and a cohesive approach towards resolving the incident and mitigating its impact.

Continuous improvement is a linchpin in the overarching framework of incident response and recovery. Post-incident reviews and debriefings enable organizations to assess response effectiveness, identify lessons learned, and refine incident response strategies iteratively.

Embracing a culture of continuous learning, adaptation, and enhancement empowers organizations to fortify their readiness, resilience, and ability to navigate the complex threat landscape adeptly, fostering a proactive stance towards safeguarding their digital assets, reputation, and operations from malevolent threats.

Emerging Trends in Cybersecurity

As technology continues to advance at an unprecedented rate, the realm of cybersecurity is witnessing a seismic shift in response to increasingly sophisticated threats and complex digital environments. In the exploration of the prevailing trends shaping the cybersecurity landscape, it becomes evident that organizations must continually evolve their security strategies to withstand the ever-evolving threat landscape.

Artificial intelligence (AI) and machine learning stand as undisputed game-changers in the cybersecurity realm, revolutionizing threat detection and response mechanisms. The deployment of AI-driven cybersecurity solutions empowers organizations to harness the power of predictive analytics, anomaly detection, and behavioral analysis to preemptively identify and neutralize potential security breaches. By automating the analysis of vast datasets in real-time, AI augments the effectiveness of cybersecurity teams in proactively defending against sophisticated cyber threats.

Moreover, the pervasive adoption of **cloud computing** has redefined traditional cybersecurity paradigms, necessitating robust cloud security measures to safeguard sensitive data stored and processed in cloud environments.

Encryption, multi-factor authentication, and continuous monitoring are indispensable components of a comprehensive cloud security strategy aimed at thwarting unauthorized access attempts, data exfiltration, and other cloud-specific security risks.

As organizations increasingly leverage cloud services to drive digital transformation, ensuring the confidentiality, integrity, and availability of cloud-hosted data is paramount.

The ubiquitous proliferation of **Internet of Things (IoT)** devices presents a growing cybersecurity challenge, as these interconnected devices often lack adequate security controls, rendering them vulnerable to exploitation by malicious actors.

Securing IoT ecosystems demands a **multi-faceted approach** encompassing device authentication, encryption protocols, regular software updates, and robust network segmentation to mitigate the risk of cyber attacks targeting IoT infrastructures.

By fortifying IoT security measures, organizations can safeguard critical systems, protect sensitive data, and uphold the privacy of end-users amidst the expanding IoT landscape.

The convergence of **IT and operational technology (OT)** networks signifies a pivotal juncture in cybersecurity considerations, highlighting the interconnectedness between digital systems and industrial control environments.

The integration of IT/OT systems necessitates **stringent security practices**, such as network segmentation, continuous monitoring, and anomaly detection, to fortify defenses against cyber threats that could disrupt operations, compromise safety, or inflict substantial economic losses.

By implementing comprehensive IT/OT security controls, organizations can bolster resilience against cyber attacks seeking to exploit vulnerabilities in interconnected digital infrastructures.

Reporting Suspicious Activities

Recognizing and reporting suspicious activities such as phishing attempts is crucial in combating cyber threats.

If you encounter any suspicious emails, websites, or phone calls, you can take the following steps:

1. Phishing Emails: If you receive a suspicious email requesting personal information or containing links to unfamiliar websites, do not click on any links or provide any sensitive information. Instead, report the email as phishing to your corporate IT Security Team and/or to your email provider. Most email services offer a "Report Phishing" option.

2. Phishing Websites: If you come across a suspicious website that appears to be phishing for personal information, you can report it to Google's Safe Browsing or other similar services. Additionally, you can notify the website's hosting provider to take action against the malicious site.

3. Phone Calls: If you receive a suspicious phone call, especially if it pertains to fraudulent activities or scams, you can report it to the Federal Communications Commission (FCC). The FCC provides an online complaint form where you can provide details about the suspicious call.

The form can be found at: **https://consumercomplaints.fcc.gov/hc/en-us**

4. Text Messages: Similarly, if you receive suspicious text messages, especially those attempting to deceive or defraud you, you can report them to the FCC using their online complaint form.

If you feel you have fallen victim to a scam, be sure to notify your local law enforcement agency right away. Especially if you have given access to your computer or your bank accounts.

And (*and I cannot stress this enough*), please help take care of our elderly family and neighbors. We need to help those that cannot help themselves.

Conclusion

The dynamic cybersecurity landscape demands continual vigilance and adaptability to counteract emerging threats and vulnerabilities in the digital realm.

By embracing cutting-edge technologies, adhering to best practices, and aligning security strategies with regulatory mandates, organizations can foster a culture of cybersecurity resilience that safeguards critical assets, protects sensitive information, and fosters trust in an increasingly interconnected and digitalized world.

By staying vigilant, helping others, and promptly reporting suspicious activities, you contribute to a safer digital environment for yourself and others.

This guide has lots of important information contained within it that can help you get on the right path to better cybersecurity and compliance.

And if you feel that you need help, there are plenty of us "Cyber Defenders" out there that stand ready to help in any way we can.

www.ingramcontent.com/pod-product-compliance
Lightning Source LLC
Chambersburg PA
CBHW070904070326
40690CB00009B/1985